TABLE OF CONTENTS

MW00568019

JOURNAL WRITING

1.	What is your favourite toy? Tell why.
2.	What is your favourite food? Tell why.
3.	What is the best part about being in your class? Tell why.
4.	What is your favourite pet? Tell why.
5.	What is your favourite zoo animal? Tell why.
6.	I wonder why...
7.	Something I am proud of is____ because...
8.	What would you like to be when you grow up? Tell why.
9.	Would you want to be a grown up? Tell why or why not.
10.	What makes you happy? Tell why.
11.	What makes you sad? Tell why.
12.	I wish I could ____ because...
13.	My favourite holiday day is ____ because...
14.	A good friend is someone who ____ because...
15.	It was really funny when ____ because...
16.	My favourite book is ____ because...
17.	I went to...
18.	A place I would like to visit is ____ because...
19.	My family is special because...
20.	If I could be an animal I would be ____ because...
21.	This weekend I want to...
22.	I am afraid of ____ because...
23.	I want to learn more about ____ because...
24.	It makes me angry when____ because...
25.	When I was a baby...
26.	What are some of your chores at home?
27.	If I could have a superpower, it would be ____ because...
28.	Would you rather be as small as a mouse or as large as a dinosaur? Tell why.
29.	How would you spend a $100?
30.	My favourite game is ____ because...

MY JOURNAL ABOUT...

_____

☐ I checked for capitals and periods.

MY READING LOG

Book Title	Author	Would you recommend this book?

READING GRAPH

Celebrate reading in your classroom with a class reading graph! Write each student's name on a cone. Each time they read a book, add an ice cream scoop to their cone.

HURRAY!
I READ A BOOK!

HURRAY!
I READ A BOOK!

HURRAY!
I READ A BOOK!

HURRAY!
I READ A BOOK!

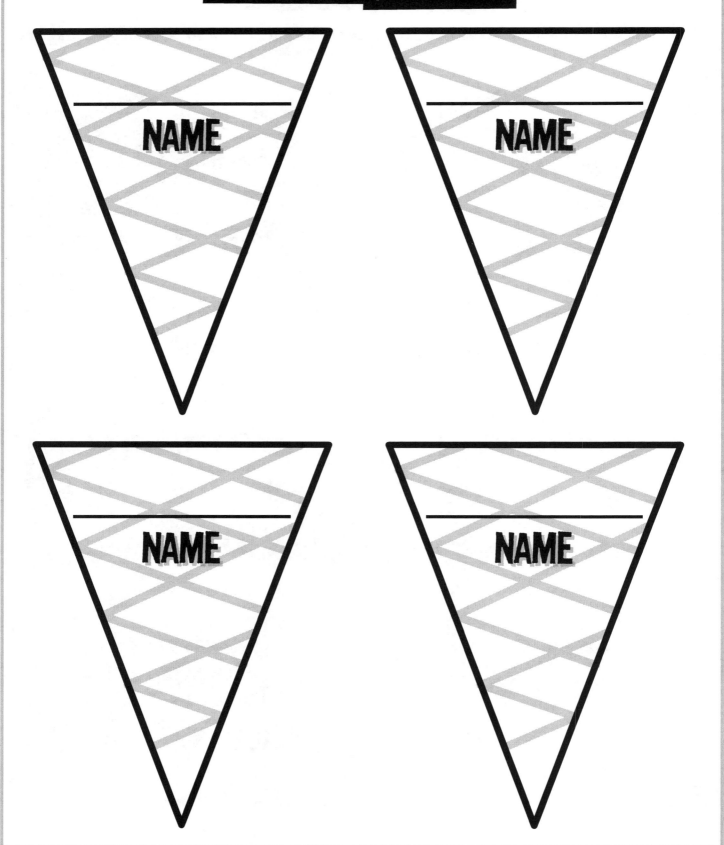

OUR CLASS NEWSLETTER

What did we do in school today?

MONDAY

TUESDAY

WEDNESDAY

THURSDAY

FRIDAY

NOTES

MY FAVOURITE PART...

Book Title: _____

This is a picture of my favourite part of the story.

The story reminds me of...

_____

_____

_____

_____

_____

_____

A WEB ABOUT...

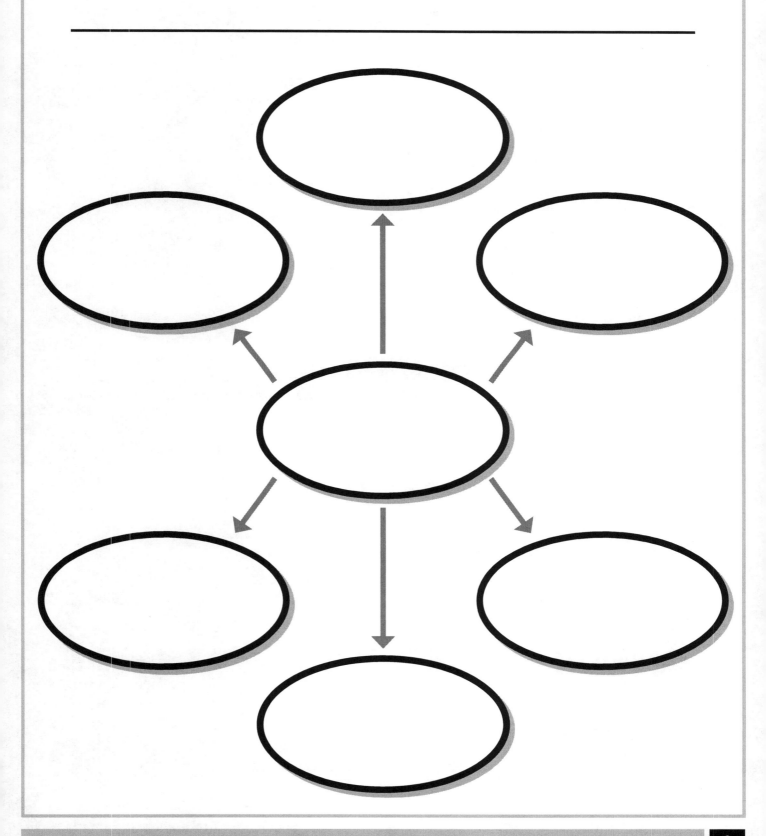

RHYMES, CHANTS AND FINGER PLAYS

Five Little Speckled Frogs

Five little speckled frogs,   *(hold up five fingers)*
Sitting on a speckled log,   *(sit down)*
Eating the most delicious bugs...yum, yum.   *(pretend to eat)*
One jumped into the pool   *(jump)*
Where it was nice and cool.
Then there were four speckled frogs.

Continue until only one frog is left.

One little speckled frog.
Sitting on a speckled log,
Eating the most delicious bugs...yum, yum.
He jumped into the pool
Where it was nice and cool.
Now there are no speckled frogs.

Hickory, Dickory, Dock

Hickory, dickory, dock,
The mouse ran up the clock;
The clock struck one,
The mouse ran down;
Hickory, dickory, dock.

Count to 100 Chant

Hooray! Hooray!
Count to 100 in different ways!

Count by 1's - its really fun!
1, 2, 3, 4, 5, ...

Count by 2's - I will count with you!
2, 4, 6, 8, 10, ...

Count by 5's - its easy if you try!
5, 10, 15, 20, 25, ...

Count by 10 and then start over again!
10, 20, 30, 40, ...

RHYMES, CHANTS AND FINGER PLAYS

Ten Fingers

I have ten fingers	*(hold up both hands showing all ten fingers)*
And they all belong to me,	*(point to self)*
I can make them do things -	*(wiggle fingers)*
Would you like to see?	*(point to eyes)*
I can shut them up tight	*(make fists)*
I can open them wide	*(open hands and spread out fingers)*
I can put them together	*(clasp hands together)*
I can make them all hide	*(put hands behind back)*
I can make them jump high	*(hold hands over head)*
I can make them jump low	*(touch the floor with all ten fingers)*
I can fold them up quietly	*(fold hands in lap)*
And hold them just so.	

Who stole the cookie from the cookie jar?

Who stole the cookie from the cookie jar?

_____ *(child's name)* stole the cookie from the cookie jar.

(named child) Who me?

(other children) Ya you!

(named child) Couldn't be!

(other children) Then who?

Repeat above verse with the name of a new child.

Tip: The teacher may wish to have a cookie jar filled with student name cards. Have a student pick a name card from the cookie jar to start the rhyme.

I'm a Little Teapot

I'm a little teapot, short and stout	*(place one hand on hip to imitate a handle)*
	(position other hand in the air to imitate a spout)
Here is my handle,	
Here is my spout.	
When I get all steamed up	
Then I shout.	
Tip me over.	*(lean to the right to imitate pouring tea from the spout)*
And pour me out!	

A WORD SEARCH ABOUT...

Create a word search and share it with your classmates.

WORD LIST

"WANTED!" POSTER

WANTED!

Who or what?

Last seen?

Description?

Wanted for?

Reward?

CATEGORY CRAZE

Encourage students to develop their categorizing skills in this fun fast-paced game.

WHAT YOU NEED:

No materials needed.

WHAT YOU DO:

1. Explain to the students that a category is a group or set of things, people, or actions that are classified together because of common characteristics. Give an example of a category and a word that belongs in it. For example, the category pets and the word dog.

2. Arrange the class into two teams. As students participate and name a word for the category they receive points for their team. Keep a tally score on the chalkboard.

3. Call out a new category when there are no more words offered by either team.

4. Set a time limit on the game and declare the winning team at the conclusion.

SAMPLE CATEGORIES:

• authors	• sports
• colours	• games
• animals	• toys
• plants	• fruits
• cities	• names
• shoes	• dwellings
• vegetables	• fish
• occupations	• birds
• vegetables	• languages
• countries	• transportation

MAKING WORDS

a

b

c

d

e

f

g

h

i

j

k

l

m	n
o	p
q	r

S	t
U	V
W	X

y

z

Match the uppercase letters to their lowercase letters.

Make rhyming words.

Line up the letters in alphabetical order.

Practice your spelling words.

A

B

C

D

E

F

G

H

I

J

K

L

M

N

O

P

Q

R

S

T

U

V

W

X

Y

Z

at

op

an

it

ed	et
ar	eg
ake	ix

ike	ock
eet	us
ug	ed

PRINTING PRACTICE

Trace the upper case alphabet.

PRINTING PRACTICE

Trace the lower case alphabet.

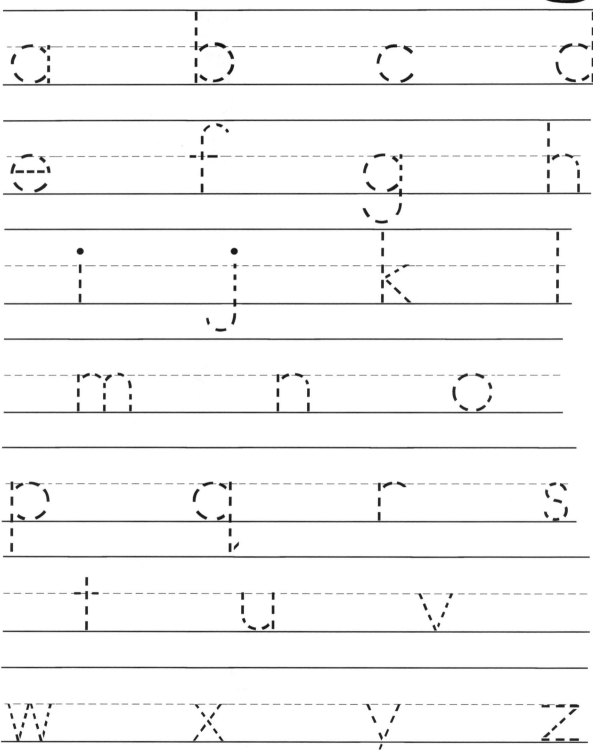

ALPHABET PRACTICE

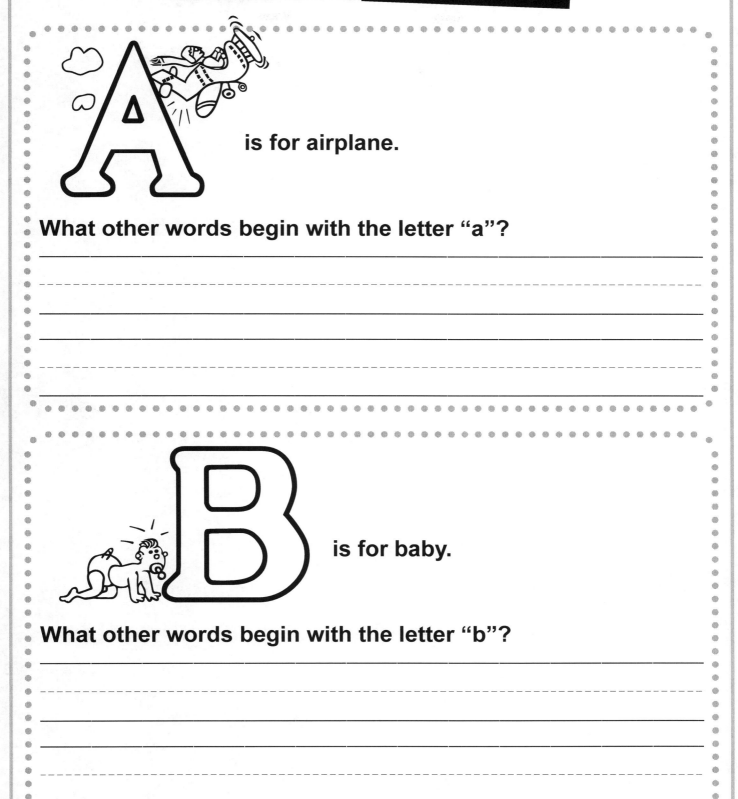

is for airplane.

What other words begin with the letter "a"?

_____

- - - - - - - - - - - - - - - - - - -

_____

_____

_____

is for baby.

What other words begin with the letter "b"?

_____

- - - - - - - - - - - - - - - - - - -

_____

_____

_____

 is for car.

What other words begin with the letter "c"?

_____

- -

_____

- -

_____

is for dinosaur.

What other words begin with the letter "d"?

_____

- -

_____

- -

_____

is for elephant.

What other words begin with the letter "e"?

_____

_____

_____

_____

is for fountain.

What other words begin with the letter "f"?

_____

_____

_____

_____

is for gorilla.

What other words begin with the letter "g"?

_____

- - - - - - - - - - - - - - - - - - -

_____

_____

_____

is for hippo.

What other words begin with the letter "h"?

_____

- - - - - - - - - - - - - - - - - - -

_____

_____

_____

ALPHABET PRACTICE

 is for igloo.

What other words begin with the letter "i"?

_____

- -

_____

- -

_____

- -

 is for jaguar.

What other words begin with the letter "j"?

_____

- -

_____

- -

_____

- -

ALPHABET PRACTICE

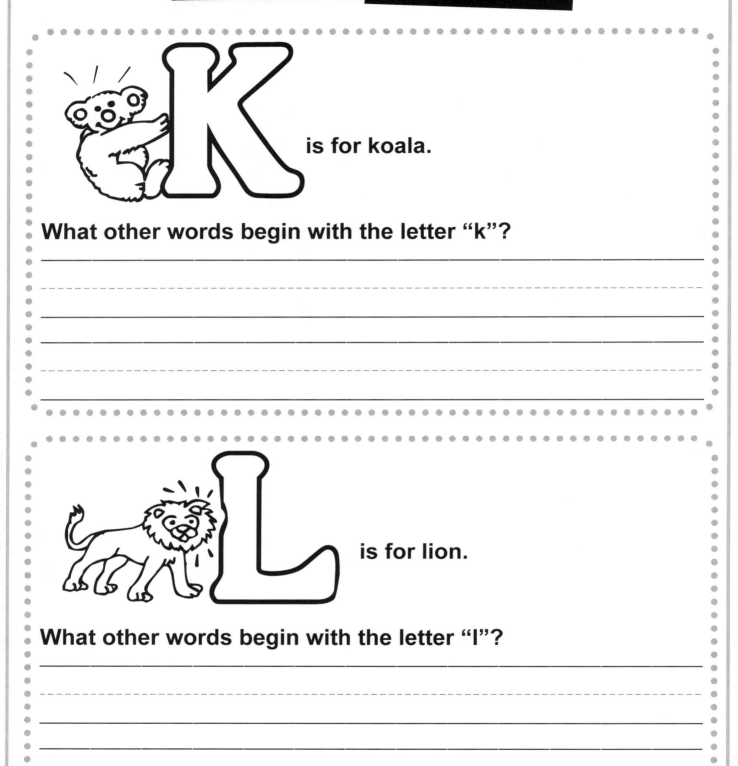

K is for koala.

What other words begin with the letter "k"?

_____

_____

_____

_____

L is for lion.

What other words begin with the letter "l"?

_____

_____

_____

_____

M is for mother.

What other words begin with the letter "m"?

_____

- -

_____

_____

- -

_____

N is for nest.

What other words begin with the letter "n"?

_____

- -

_____

_____

- -

_____

is for opera.

What other words begin with the letter "o"?

_____

_____

_____

_____

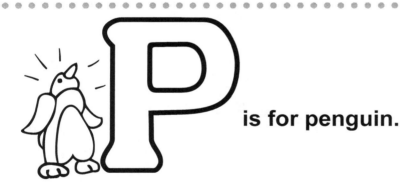

is for penguin.

What other words begin with the letter "p"?

_____

_____

_____

_____

is for quintet.

What other words begin with the letter "q"?

_____

_____

_____

_____

is for robot.

What other words begin with the letter "r"?

_____

_____

_____

_____

S is for sun.

What other words begin with the letter "s"?

_____

_____

_____

_____

T is for turtle.

What other words begin with the letter "t"?

_____

_____

_____

_____

ALPHABET PRACTICE

U is for unicorn.

What other words begin with the letter "u"?

_____

_____

_____

_____

V is for viking.

What other words begin with the letter "v"?

_____

_____

_____

_____

ALPHABET PRACTICE

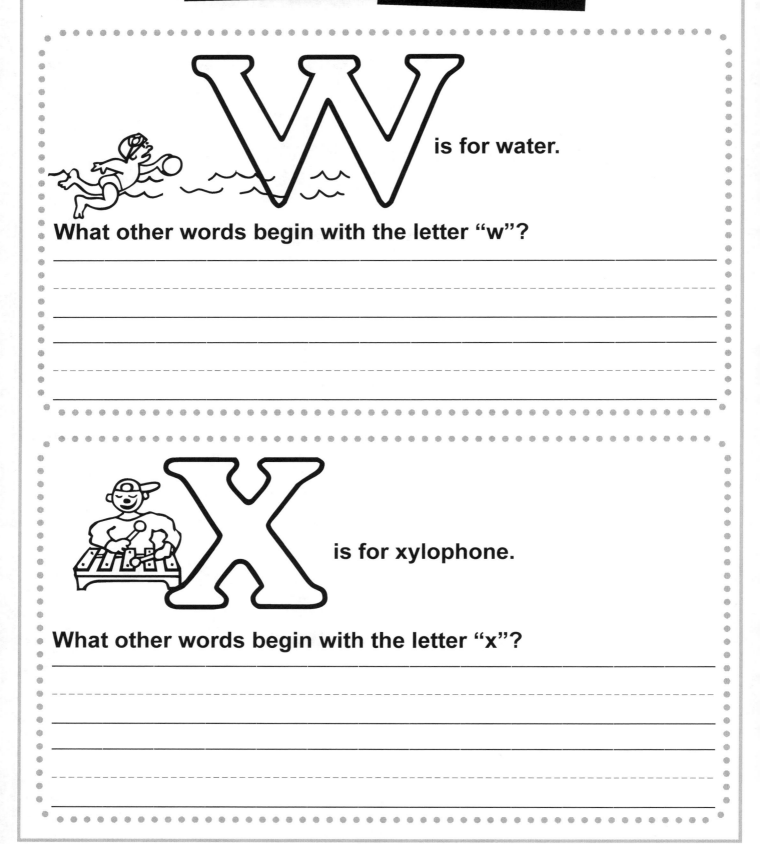

W is for water.

What other words begin with the letter "w"?

_____

_____

_____

_____

X is for xylophone.

What other words begin with the letter "x"?

_____

_____

_____

_____

Y is for yo-yo.

What other words begin with the letter "y"?

Z is for zoo.

What other words begin with the letter "z"?

triangle

square

circle

rectangle

pentagon

hexagon

SUPER SHAPE CONCENTRATION

octagon

parallelogram

trapezoid

SUPER SHAPE CONCENTRATION

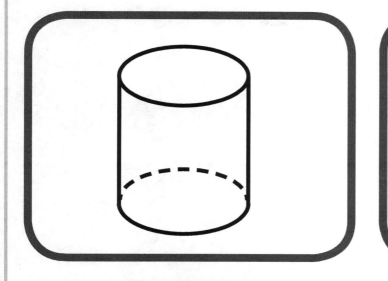

cylinder

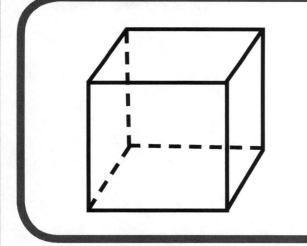

cube

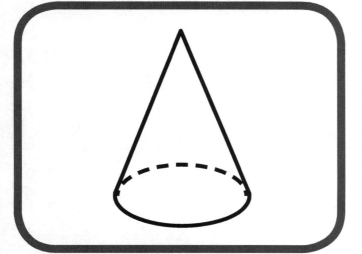

cone

SUPER SHAPE CONCENTRATION

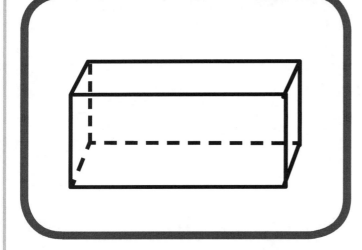

rectangular prism

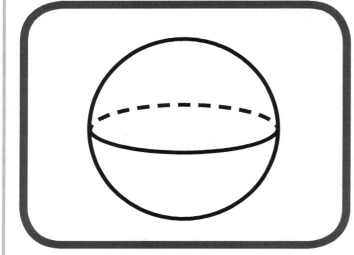

sphere

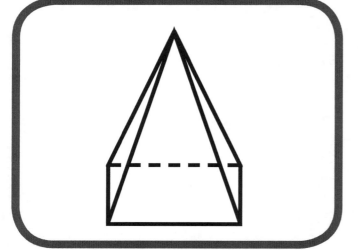

pyramid

GEOMETRIC CANADIAN BEAVER

Demonstrate for students how geometric shapes can be used to make organic forms. For example, to make eyes you can use a circle.

This activity works best when children have an adult present to guide them. Before assembling the beaver, have students carefully cut out their shapes.

Children may use the shapes on the next two pages as tracers, or cut the shapes and colour or paint them.

1. Model for children how to glue the two largest brown circles, overlapping on top of each other resembling a figure eight.	
2. Next, for the beaver ears glue two small ovals onto the top of the head. 3. Add and glue the small square beaver teeth at the bottom of the head.	
4. For the beaver muzzle, glue two medium brown circles. 5. For the eyes, first glue the white ovals above the muzzle. Lastly, place the two black circles on top of the white ovals.	

PERFECT PATTERNS

1. Draw what comes next in the pattern.
2. Make your own colour pattern for each row.

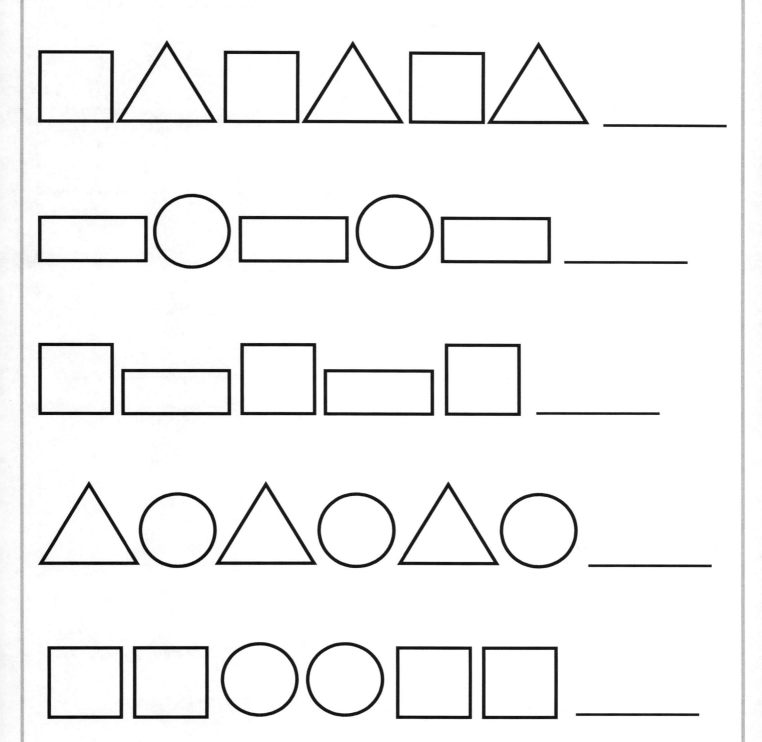

SUPER SHAPES

Trace and practice drawing the shapes.

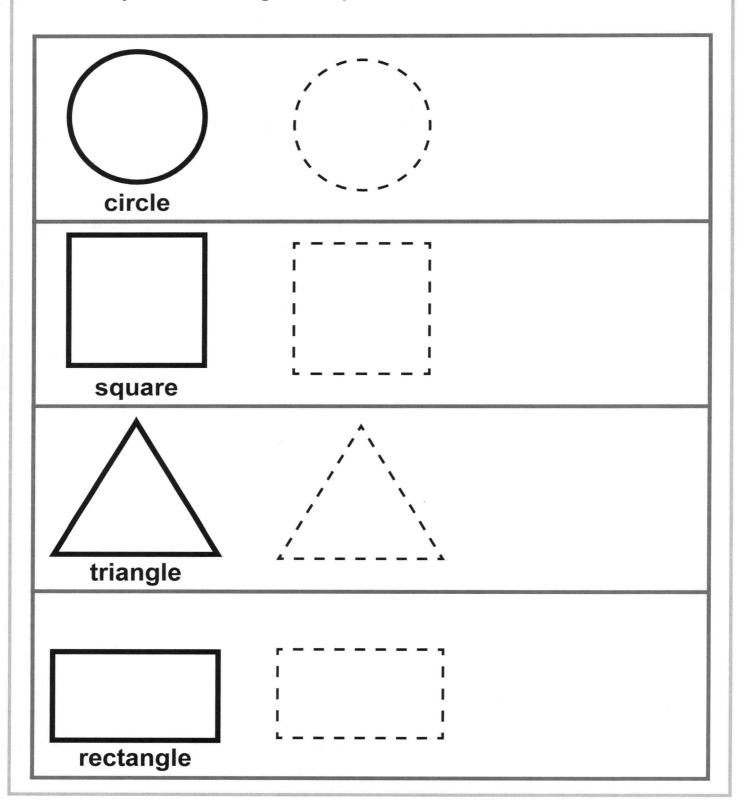

circle

square

triangle

rectangle

COUNT AND WRITE

Look at the picture. How many of each animal?

Complete the 100 chart.

1									10
	12								
							28		
31									
				45					
						57			60
71								79	
		83							
								99	

Count by 1's. Colour the number pattern in red.

Count by 2's. Colour the number pattern in blue.

Count by 5's. Mark the number pattern with green X's.

Count by 10's. Circle the numbers in orange.

Draw coins to show different ways to make 10 ¢.

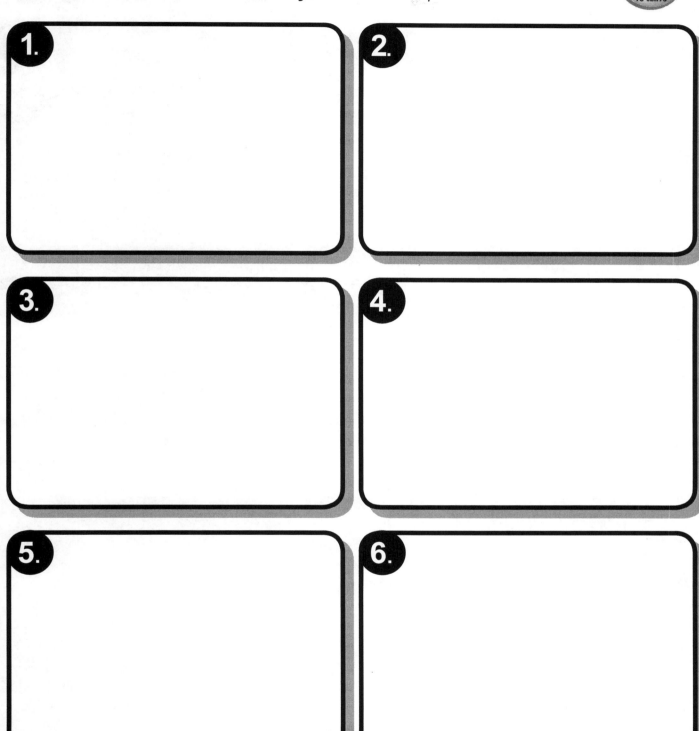

1.

2.

3.

4.

5.

6.

LET'S MAKE 25¢

Draw coins to show different ways to make 25 ¢.

1.

2.

3.

4.

5.

6.

COIN MATCH

penny

nickel

dime

quarter

loonie

toonie

SUPER SHAPE ARTIST

Use the shapes to draw a picture.

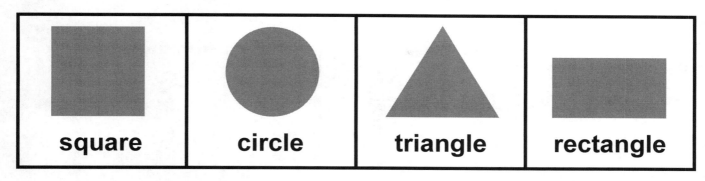

| square | circle | triangle | rectangle |

In my picture I have:

_____   _____   _____   _____

Create a bookmark, cut it out, fold in half and glue together!

GET TO KNOW YOUR COLOURS

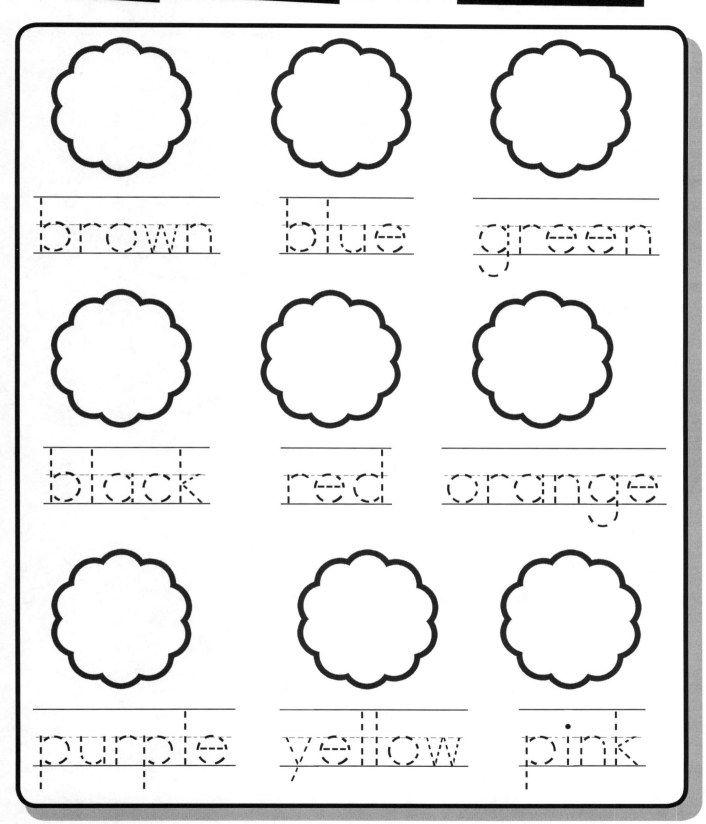

brown blue green

black red orange

purple yellow pink

COLOUR THE CLOWN!

CANADIAN FLAG

Canada's flag is a red flag with a single, red maple leaf on a white square. Colour the flag.

Create your own personal flag.

Chalkboard Publishing © 2008

CREATE A STAMP

Create a stamp.

Write about your stamp:

_____

_ _

_____

Design your own Canadian $1.00 coin.

This is what a real $1.00 coin looks like!

The nickname for the Canadian $1.00 coin is the loonie. What is the nickname of your $1.00 coin and why?

_____

- -

_____

DRAW A PORTRAIT

Draw a portrait of a family member, friend, or pet .

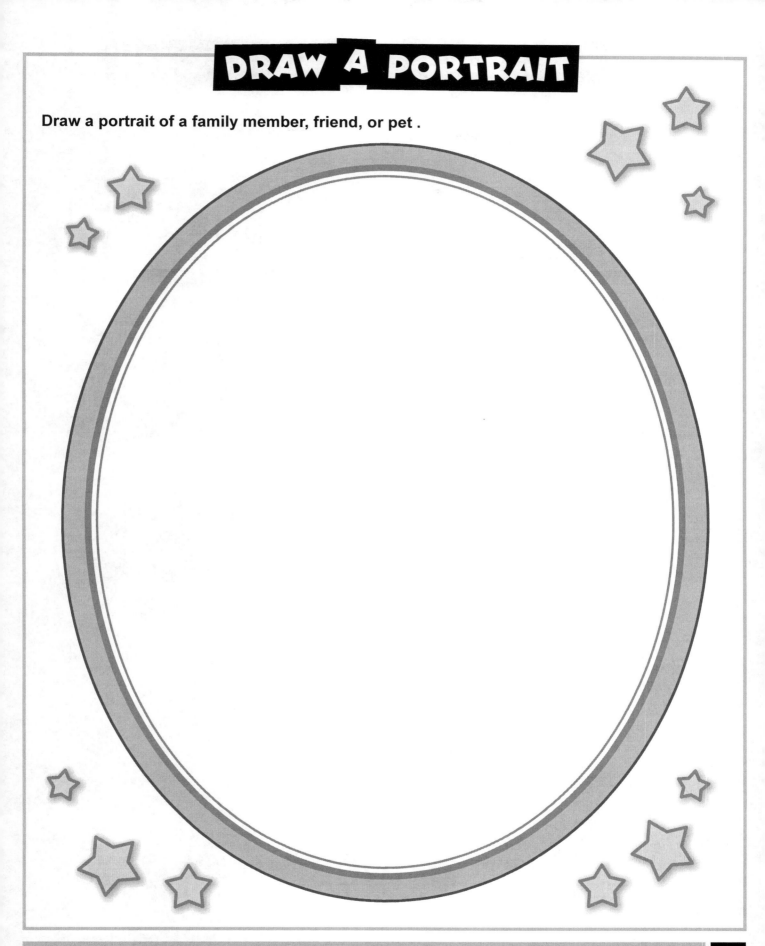

NOSE

EYES

DESIGN YOUR OWN CHARACTER

HAIR

MOUTH

CONNECT THE DOTS

Connect the dots by following the numbers. Colour the picture.

START
HERE

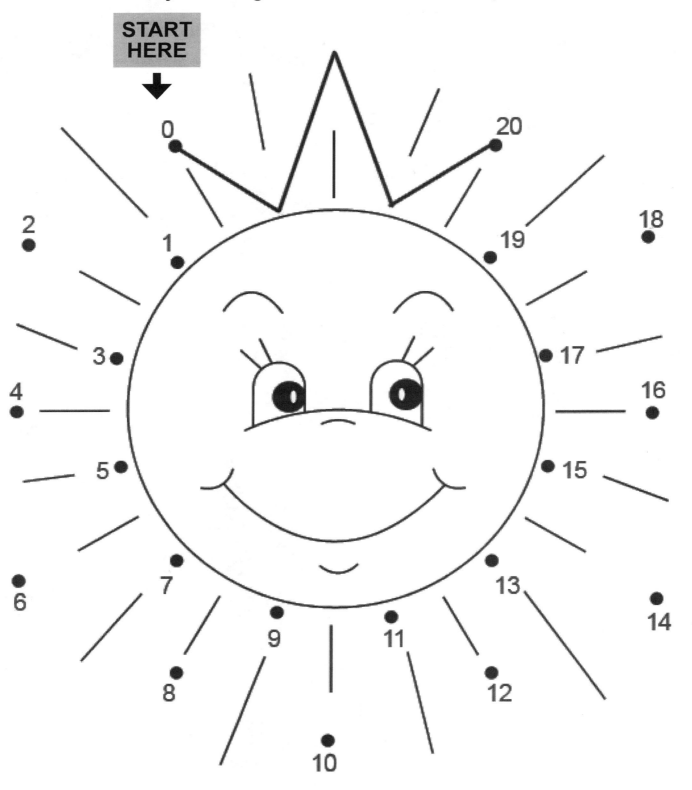

CONNECT THE DOTS

Connect the dots by following the numbers. Colour the picture.

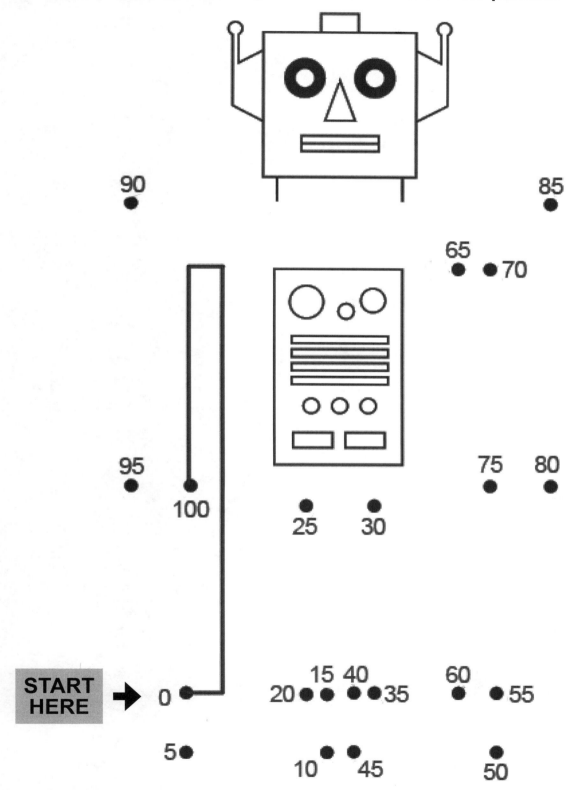

90

85

65

70

95

100

75   80

25   30

START
HERE

0

15 40

20   35

60

55

5

10   45

50

CONNECT THE DOTS

Connect the dots by following the numbers. Colour the picture.

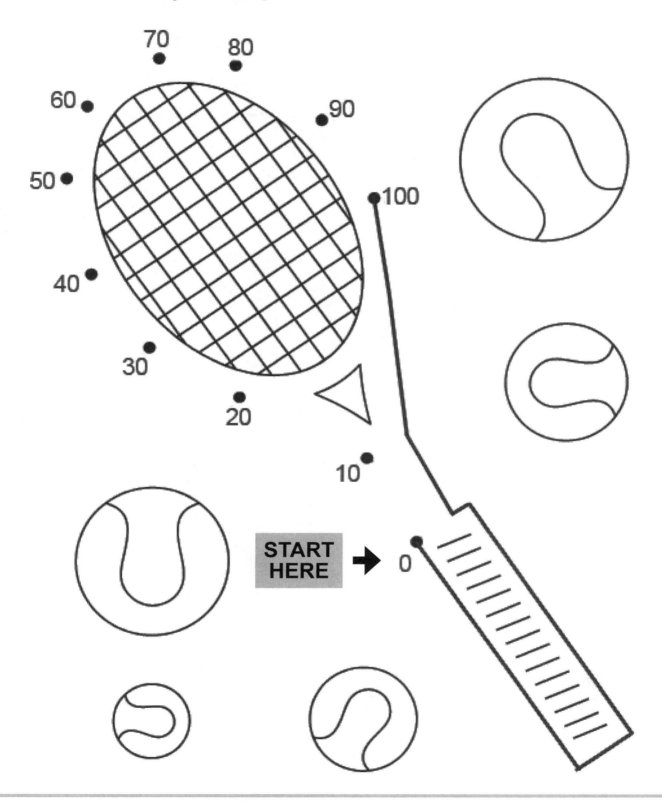

START HERE ➔ 0

Connect the dots by following the ABCs. Colour the picture.

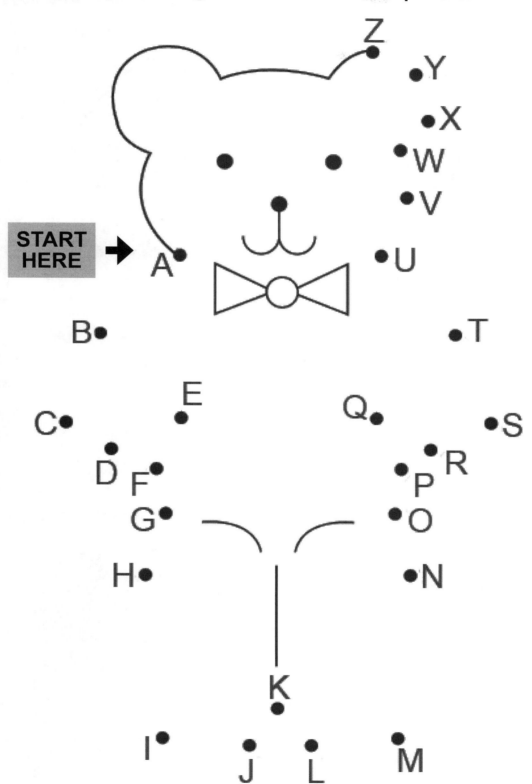

START HERE →

Find the football.

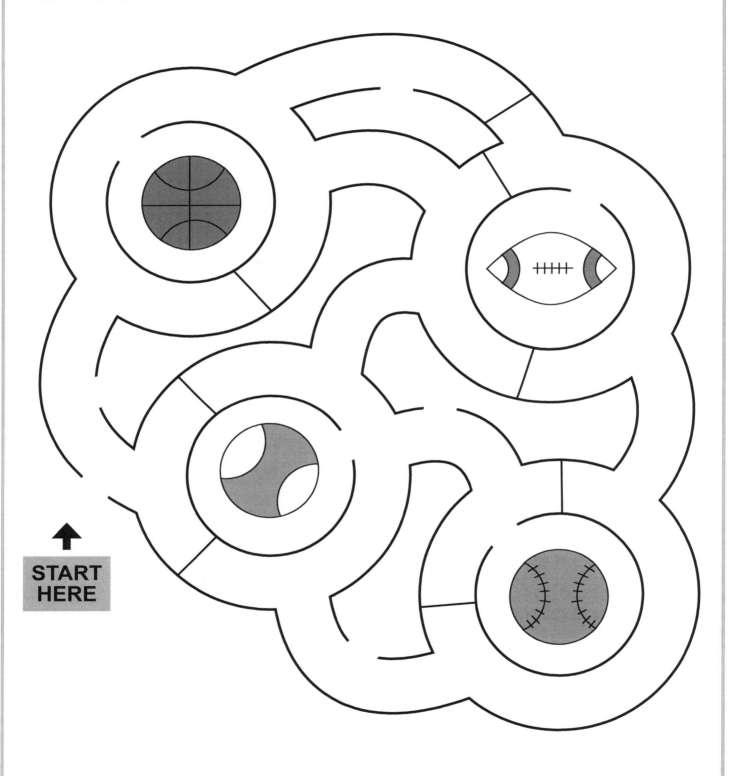

START
HERE

MYSTERY MAZE

Find the bee, then colour the picture.

START HERE

CRAZY COLOURING IDEAS

As a great time filler, have children practice their fine motor skills using different media to colour colouring pages or simple geometric shapes.

Colour a colouring page or large geometric shapes:

- on different surfaces such as sand paper to create interesting textures

- alternating heavy and light strokes

- using only primary colours

- using only secondary colours

- using different shades of the same colour

- with different colours of chalk and setting it with hair spray

- using pastels

- using watercolours

- vertical lines

- horizontal lines

Fill in sections of a colouring page or geometric shape using:

- different colours of plastiscene

- tiny bits of torn construction paper

- mixed media

- different colours of thick yarn

- different patterns

- cotton swab dots

Chalkboard Publishing © 2008

DIRECT DRAW

Encourage students to think of art as the personal interpretation of ideas. This is a quick art activity that demonstrates for students how, with the same directions, each student's execution of those directions is unique. At the end of the activity, collect all of the students' art and create a wonderful display of abstract art based on shape, colour and line.

WHAT YOU NEED:

- piece of square paper
- colouring materials

WHAT YOU DO:

1. Instruct students to follow the directions in order to complete a piece of art.

2. Take a survey of the class to predict if they think all of students' artwork will look the same if everyone follows the same directions.

3. Next call out directions such as the following:
    - draw a thin line across the page.
    - draw a thick line across the page.
    - draw a circle anywhere on your paper.
    - draw a triangle somewhere on your paper.
    - directions of your choice that will reinforce art vocabulary.

4. Once the directions are called out, have students compare their artwork with a partner, focusing on how the art pieces are the same or different.

5. Display the students' artwork as a combined piece of group art.

 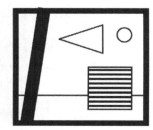 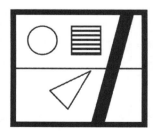 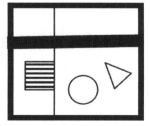

TIC TAC TOE

Get three X's in a row (horizontal, vertical, or diagonal) before your partner gets three O's in a row.

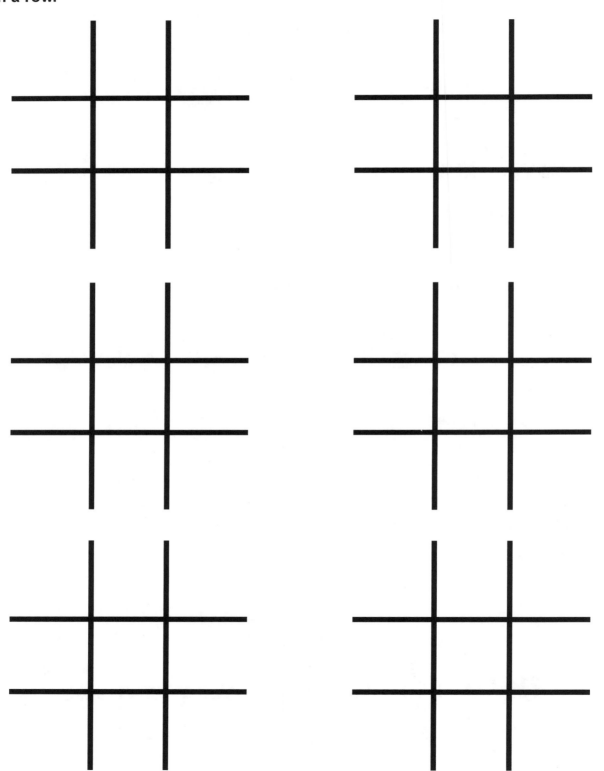

SUPER SMELLY PLAYDOUGH

Create a playdough centre in your classroom and use it as a springboard to develop modelling, fine motor, language and number skills.

Ingredients:

- 3 cups of flour
- ½ cup of salt
- 2 packages of flavoured drink crystals
- 2 cups boiling water

What To Do:

1. Mix dry ingredients in a bowl.
2. Add boiling water.
3. Mix and knead on a floured surface.
4. Store in an air tight container.

Playdough Manipulatives:

Here are some items to have on hand for students to use at the playdough centre:

- items to imprint with such as cut up veggies and fruit, seashells and leaves
- cookie cutters
- rolling pin
- plastic spoons, forks, and knives
- containers of different shapes and sizes
- a bowl of water

Encourage Students To:

- Create playdough snakes and form letters of the alphabet.
- Use playdough letters to form words.
- Mould different objects.

MORE TIME FILLER IDEAS

1. Daily Physical Exercise

Take a few minutes as a class and do some kind of physical activity. It can be anything from a stretch to challenging students to see how many jumping jacks, pushups etc they can do in one minute. Students also enjoy doing aerobics to music.

2. Classroom Cleanup

Challenge students to pick up, straighten, or put away 10 things in the classroom in 100 seconds.

3. Broken Telephone

Broken telephone is a fantastic game that students never tire of in which each successive student whispers to the next a phrase or sentence whispered to them by the preceding student. As the message is communicated, cumulative errors from mishearing often happen and consequently the sentence heard by the last player is completely different.

4. Board Games

Have a supply of games on hand for students to play such as *Snakes and Ladders* or *Scrabble*.

5. Joke or Riddle of the Day

Keep a list of jokes and riddle books handy to share with the class.

6. Class Messages

Class Messages are an excellent way to provide students with interesting facts about the theme they are studying while also arranging teachable moments in the use of grammar and punctuation. Write a class message in a letter format with grammatical and punctuation errors. Then have students help you edit the message. Once completely edited, use the class message as a springboard for a class discussion.

7. What Did We Learn in School Today?

Keep parents informed about class happenings with this easy weekly newsletter! Take a few minutes at the end of each school day and ask students what they learned in school. Record each comment in the appropriate day of the week box on the blackline master found in this book. The teacher may wish to also record a student's initials after each comment. Use the notes box to recommend a website or to remind parents about important information.

8. Share Personal Happenings

Have students share personal happenings in their lives.

9. Learning Logs

Have students keep a learning log to fill out whenever they have some spare time. This is not only a time filler, but is an effective way for a teacher to gain insight as to what a student has learned or is thinking about. Learning logs can include the following:

- teacher prompts
- student personal reflections
- questions that arise
- connections discovered
- labeled diagrams and pictures

10. Working with Letters

Have children work alone or with a partner to:

- match uppercase letters to lowercase letters.
- place the letters in the order of the alphabet.
- play variations of *Concentration*.
- manipulate letters and create word families.

11. Listening Centre

A listening centre is always a favourite. Students can listen to and read along with a story.

12. Drama Centre

A drama centre in your class will promote students' practice of language skills through the communication of ideas and dramatic play. Set up a drama centre to represent a specific place in your community. Encourage students to bring in items that can represent places in the community.

For example:

- Post Office – provide items like stamps, envelopes, a class mailbox, and assign a postal worker to deliver class mail.
- Hospital - provide a play medical kit, and medical masks.
- Restaurant - provide a table, chairs, plastic cutlery, paper cups and plates, plastic food, also have students come up with a class café menu.

WEBSITES FOR KIDS

STARFALL   www.starfall.com

This is a fantastic interactive website that helps teach children to read. Ideal for kindergarten and first grade. Encourage students to explore many worthwhile activities such as exciting interactive books and phonics games.

MAGIC KEYS   www.magickeys.com/books/index.html

This is great website where students can read stories online.

CREATE A CHARACTER

www.bgfl.org/bgfl/custom/resources_ftp/client_ftp/ks1/english/characters/notes.htm

This is a unique interactive website where students create their own character and then have a chance to describe it. Students choose the type of clothes, hair and skin colour that they want the character to have. Once complete students can click on the Print button at the top of the screen and the character and sentences about the character will be printed.

FUN SCHOOL   http://funschool.kaboose.com/preschool/

This is a first rate website for young children. Encourage students to try the online games and activities for preschool kids like coloring pages, counting games, and alphabet games.

MISTER ROGERS NEIGHBOURHOOD   http://pbskids.org/rogers/

The Mister Rogers Neighourhood website has sections where children can build their own neighbourhood or take a factory tour to see how things are made.

AAA MATH   www.aaamath.com

This impressive website features a comprehensive set of interactive arithmetic lessons. Unlimited practice is available on each topic which encourage thorough mastery of different math concepts.

TVO KIDS   www.tvokids.com

This Canadian website offers children from ages three through eight years old fun, engaging and educational activities.

I KNOW THAT   www.iknowthat.com

This website is always a favourite with students! It offers educational activities that include sticker books, simulation games, painting, math and phonics.